Fly Sandwich

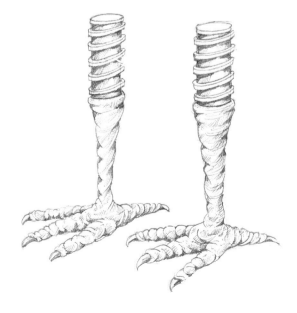

Ivor Cutler
and
Martin Honeysett

FLY SANDWICH
and other menu

Methuen

Other books by Ivor Cutler

Poetry
Private Habits (*Arc*)
Large et Puffy (*Arc*)
Fresh Carpet (*Arc*)
A Nice Wee Present
   from Scotland (*Arc*)
Terrific Fun (*Arc*)

Children's Books
Herbert – Five Stories
(*illustrated by Patrick Benson*)
Grape Zoo
(*illustrated by Jill Barton*)
Meal One
(*illustrated by Helen Oxenbury*)
The Animal House
(*illustrated by Helen Oxenbury*)

Records
Privilege (*Rough Trade*)
Jammy Smears (*Virgin*)
Velvet Donkey (*Virgin*)
Dandruff (*Virgin*)
Life in a Scotch Sitting Room
   Vol II (*SpeakOut*)
Prince Ivor (*Rough Trade*)

with Martin Honeysett
Gruts
Fremsley
Life in a Scotch
   Sitting Room Vol II
Glasgow Dreamer

Other books by Martin Honeysett

'Private Eye' Cartoonists:
   No. 4 Martin Honeysett
   (*Deutsch/Private Eye*)
Honeysett at Home
   (*Dempsey and Squires*)
The Motor Show Book of Humour
   (*Gresham*)
Microphobia (*Century*)
Fit for Nothing (*Century*)
The Not Another Book of
   Old Photographs Book
Dr Fegg's Encyclopeadia of
   All World Knowledge (*illus*)
Animal Nonsense Rhymes

First published in
Great Britain in 1991
by Methuen
Michelin House,
81 Fulham Road,
London sw3 6rb

Text copyright © 1973,
1977, 1981, 1984, 1986,
1988, 1991 by Ivor Cutler

Illustrations
copyright © 1991
by Martin Honeysett

A CIP catalogue record
for this book is available
from the British Library
ISBN 0 413 65940 2

Some of these poems have
previously appeared in
the following publications:
Many flies have feathers
and *A Flat Man*, both published
by Trigram Press.
*Private Habits, Large et
Puffy, Fresh Carpet* and
A Nice Wee Present from Scotland,
all published by Arc
Publications.

Printed and bound
in Great Britain
by Clays Ltd, St Ives plc

Contents

I see the moth move
but I do not know
what it is doing.

A Shy Lark

Did you hear the lark? No. I saw him on the sky. It was so empty I joined him but he was shy and drifted off, so I sit on the grass. It is flat now, but will rise when I go. We do not praise grass enough. There goes the lark, pursued by a deaf hawk. What a menacing shadow it makes. A lark should carry a revolver.

Leopard Crossing

'Mum, must I?' 'Yes. Whoever heard of a leopard crossing the veldt without its skin? How would the other creatures know what you are?' 'But it's dark, and if I ran alongside of you they'd know I'd have to be a leopard else you'd eat me. It's hot, Mum.' 'Come here. Ptu ptu! There. Now get into your skin. There's a clean one on the chest of drawers and I don't want to hear another word.'

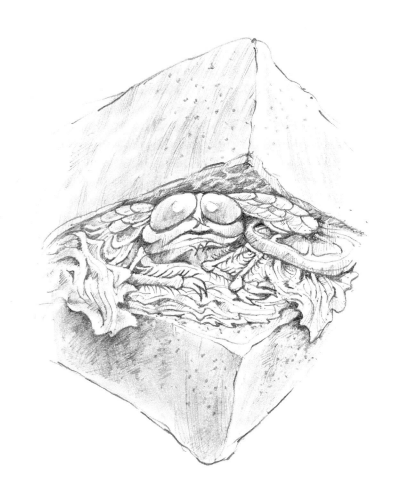

Fly Sandwich

A fly crouching in a
sandwich cannot
comprehend why it
has become more
than ordinarily
vulnerable.

Over my skin is written
history – etched events. A
yellow butterfly landed on
my rump and stayed awhile
for warmth and sweetness,
and to hear me moving
around. I have held my
cheek against a large tree
and our sap ran in the same
direction. Emotion is my
wisest tool and I use it
quietly and subtly for none
to guess. Men feel peace
easing into their twisted
heads. I am most elegant
and I love myself.

Not Many Flies

Not
many flies
have
feathers.

Unexpected Join

The
earth
meets the
sky over
the
hill.

I was
told
by
a sparrow with
a lump on
its head.

A Friendly Smell

Two sheep were sent to ask
me to join the club.
Diffident, they stood at the
fence, their whole body
moving as they breathed, a
friendly smell, willing me to
be a sheep. 'It'll do you
good,' they baaed. Then
moved away, to show me
how lonely I was.

But there was a Soay ram, a
bully, and I thought, 'Oh
no! What's the point. I may
as well stay as I am.'

Big Mice

Big mice
have
big teeth.

Tilt

I am an albatross
living inside the
body of a humorist.
One of God's little
jokes. See the look
on my face, the tilt of
my pelvis.

Drum Skin

In the sun a dove lands on a
drum's skin to listen. The
drummer slowly turns the
drum till the creature's beak
faces the afternoon. They
both dream of other matters.
Their smiles are reflected in
a shaving mirror propped
outside a wide tent.

A soldier's trumpet sends
her to a tree.

Claw Polish

A man held a hen near his
shoes to clean them with its
wings as they flapped
about. The hen enjoyed the
smell of claw polish. He had
never seen a man with bare
feet and thought boots were
human claws even though
he'd seen leather being
pulled off oxen like tight
jerseys off soccer players.
The man set the hen back
over its egg with brown
wings and strode off to the
disco to chat up a girl
because his wife had died
and he had to start all over.

Filthy My Fangs

A conservatively dressed
humble fly lurched against a
web. 'Anybody home?' Mrs
Spider sighed, laid aside her
reading specs, her red
leather edition of the Bible
according to St Septimus
and tripped along the wire,
more out of curiosity than
hunger, sucking an old bit
of caddis out from between
her fangs, to the enormous
drunken bug, pulsing
slowly, and smelling faintly
of Saturday night vomit.
'Get the hell off my web!'
she chirped. 'Go and sleep it
off, you blundering booby.
I'm not going to filthy my
fangs on you,' busily tying
him up. She'd let him go
later, after sucking him dry.
Meanwhile she'd finish the
chapter. Fatty would keep.

For a Lark

One night, for a lark, we
inverted all the trees in the
park. It was spring, and we
could hear the fledglings
chirping 20 feet below the
earth, delighted to be close
to their food supply. The
park keeper nearly had a fit,
but he was both a fatalist
and an ecologist so he just
changed the name of the
park and took notes. That
year, the sparrows grew to
the size of small ostriches.

She pushed the tea chest across the ice. Her arms sparkled with frost. Her legs were so covered with goose-pimples it was hard for the frost to get a grip and make them sparkle too.

Soon she came to the frozen grass and couldn't push the chest any further because the grass resisted it. The fog wasn't helping either.

She emptied the chest – it was full of gold bars – and pushed it to the empty cottage. 'No one will steal gold in this weather,' she thought. But a passing column of ants carried the bullion away to their hill and the little girl was shot for negligence. It was so cold in her cotton dress and clear plastic sandals she was glad to be dead.

Fish
are not
very bright
not
by my
standards.
They
never had any
reason to grow
brains. For
one thing
it's hard
to read
under water and
the paper gets too wet
to handle and
there isn't the light and
fins let books slip and you'd
have to hold the
pen in your mouth.

People
who say
'A school of fish'
are
taking
advantage of
their limited
intelligence to poke cruel
fun.

You let
fish be.

Or eat them.

A Pragmatist

A small mouse beckons a
large hornet. 'Teach me to
fly.' Earnestly, he listens to
a boring tale on instinctive
technique, then, a
pragmatist, launches into
the air, to be punched to the
ground by a bat. '. . . and
keep your place, buster!'

Buffet

A lady found an insect on her body. Fainting with disgust and observing she was alone she fetched it a slap. Shocked by the buffet it limped off to die in a dark place between her shoulder-blades out of reach. There was quite a little community there, mostly daddy-long-legs and moths, either crippled or convalescent. 'Talk about using a steamhammer to crack a nut,' they mumbled or buzzed, incensed by her rough and ready behaviour.

Deductive Lepidopteron

The
lime-coloured
listening moth
perched
in my ear
hears
the fine harmonics
which
my rubbery drum is
unable to
respond to
and bounces back.

This
gives her,
aurally, a
distorted understanding but
one
she prefers
as
it is based
on the rejections
of my older ears.
By
thinking the opposite of
what she hears,
a
fairly accurate picture grows,
considered and
reliable
for her needs,
which are
unknown
to us.

She often
sits by mistake
in seashells then
flies around in a stupid
uninformed manner.
Mostly
the chambered nautilus which
she thinks is
a
posh hotel.

Frustration

The dog stood in the mud
unable to move flashing its
teeth. The angry man with
the torn trousers stepped
briskly away humming
tightly. The amused young
woman in her see-through
baby-doll touched by the
dog's frustration threw her
cat out the window on to
the mud beside it switched
on her favourite mindless
rubbish and lifted her nail-
varnish from the padded
dressing table.

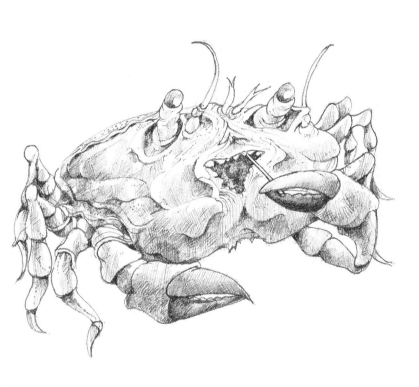

A Black Snake

A black snake writhes along
the river bottom. Old plants
watch. Vigorous fry circle
long puddles, prey to juicy
birds. Two crabs pinch a
sparrow who fell in and
snapped a pale ankle.
Tumbleweed thunders along
– grey ballbearings – off to
the sea for a holiday. A
black snake spies the damp
hole where a vole lived and
curls in, leaving two
moonstones to guard. Dark
falls. Only fish sleep. The
crabs lean back, burp and
pick their teeth.

The Two Coy Hinnies

I own a large sloping field.
People send me their mules
to cure. They enter at the
top and stand. I tell them
the joke about the two coy
hinnies and when they are
helpless with laughter, give
them a push. They run to
the bottom then bite the
fence in a fury. The field is
on a turntable and during
the night I turn it through a
straight angle.* You should
see their faces when they
wake up. I tell them the
hinny joke – it is the only
mule joke there is – and
push them. After a year,
they are thoroughly
disorientated and on
returning to their owners
are placid and biddable.

* *180 degrees or half a
revolution*

A halibut fell in love with an
albatross and tried to rub its
scales against the great bird.
The bird was shy, and
hovered. The halibut lay in
its shadow and yearned;
listened to the stinging wind
as it swept at the surface. It
learned the bird's song and
they sang duets in their
South Atlantic territory,
even when the sun was
elsewhere, for one can sing
in the dark. A man on a
whaler shot the albatross for
practice and the halibut ate
it for a momento.

He sliced mutton bones into
buttons with a tenon saw,
then buffed them till they
glowed like Baltic amber.
Girls discovered that a
licked finger rubbed round
and round could coax out a
bleat – the larger the button,
the deeper the bleat. They
invented games like 'Lost in
the Welsh hills', or
'Slaughterhouse', which
required many buttons of
different sizes and lots of
saliva. This allowed them to
exercise their talent for
empathy, and groups of
girls could be found in the
playground, rubbing
furiously and crying
piteously. Headmistresses
found the game morbid and
hypocritical, banned it and
confiscated the buttons,
often trying them out in the
privacy of their studies.
In Dorset, a purblind
sheepdog came across a
flock of girls rubbing
buttons and drove them into
their pen.

The Keeper

The keeper overwound the
small birds so they live too
quickly. Their tight jet eyes
beg to be slowed, to be
given time to consider.
Consider, with a brain the
size of a halibut liver oil
capsule. No hands. No
holidays. Just being alive
and following your nature.

If you are bitten by a killer
bee, bite it right back. A
series of alkaline antibodies
will be released which you
may spit on to the wound,
neutralising it. There is also
the keen satisfaction of
biting its furry little body in
two.

Why do I look at the stone –
draw it? Why do I stand
apart? I shall speak to it.
'Hello, stone. How are you?'
'Well, I have a little pain at
the back. It's the damp. A
little moss gathering at the
crack. Can you see?' I bend.
'Yes, I see,' but do not offer
advice. A cat is also talking
to the stone about tinned
food and the stone seems
very interested. 'Goodbye,' I
say. The stone and the cat
turn and nod. 'Come again
soon,' says the stone. What
a bloody cheek! 'Come again
soon!' A stone! In front of a
cat!

A horde of flies
with black feathers
landed silently
in winter
and
ate the crop.

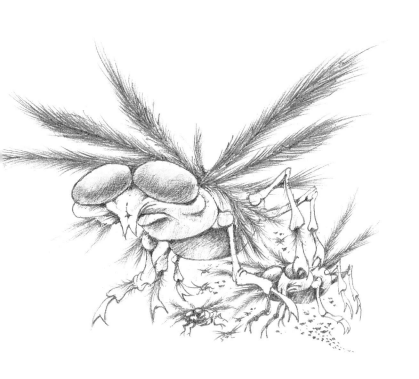

O Quartz

Sand is blowing, i.e. stones
are blowing. A minute
insect cries – stones are
blowing! – or boulders even.
So if a grain of sand hits you
it's like being hit by a house.
Sandflies are the bravest
creatures on the world.
They pray to the wind god
to let up and their worst
oath is – O quartz!

One evening, out for a fly in the sky, I was gulped down a redstart's throat. It was nearly dark. I tried to back out, but it kept gulping and gulping till I got tired and sleepy, and gave in. Its stomach smelt faintly of pickles, and that was my last memory.

Bird Rain

Birds rained into the water,
gulped at nervously by
shining grey fish. Vacuums
appeared in the air so they
fell. Fierce birds, eagles and
falcons as well. Dodos and
moas toppled in. Herring
did particularly well but
flounders got their share. I'll
never forget the surprise on
an ostrich's beak.

Just as a fish is eaten, it
shrugs. This is known as the
shrug of resignation. Fish
know they will be eaten.
They just prefer it to be later
than sooner. Krill do not
shrug when swallowed by
whales because they are
unaware of what has
happened, except it is
darker, like the cinema, and
there's a funny warm smell.
Fish do not understand the
concept of death. Try as you
will, you will not find the
word 'death' in any fish
dictionary. Is there
something in this for us to
learn?

The Wren

The wren hopped
around the cat's
tongue looking for
the exit. 'Wait till I
get back,' she
thought, 'I shall have
a tale to relate.'

Still Sore

The old moose skidded
about the prairie over the
slippery grass, dewy and
blue under the large pitted
moon. 'Where's ma baby?'
she bellowed hoarsely,
panting and sweaty. The
bull held still by a small
grove, eyes closed to avoid
lunar reflection. Sex was the
last activity – it was 3 a.m.
prairie time – that he cared
to contemplate, still sore
from a hard day's mating.

He tied the herring to a tree
by its tail and watched it,
with a mixture of curiosity
and indifference, suffocate
to death.

Don't worry, said Saint Peter
to the furious fish,
that lad will die violently.
Mollified, the herring swam
over to God for a blessing.

Potato Tune

A horse munches a field.
Early evening fetches out
singing potatoes. Carrots
listen, revolving in their
living quarters. I push a
wicket-keeper's glove into
the horizon, catch the sun,
hold the day, hear potato
tune for ever.

Wild Hens

As the wild hens wheeled
and swooped over him, he
observed tranquilly the neat
way God had screwed in
their legs like spark-plugs,
then they dived and bore
him unresisting and full of
curiosity to their great group
nest on an aspen, and laid
him over thousands of
peeping chicks. Fair do's he
thought, as their gelatinous
beaks bit away his soft life.

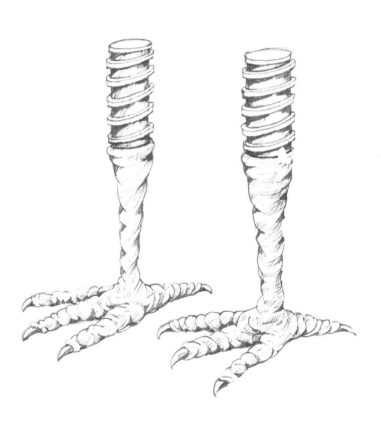

In the garden, murder is
going on. I can hear the little
shrieks. Plants are slower so
their cries are part of the
silence, which is not silence
at all. It is not very nice to
go round at night killing in
the dark. Owls are not the
kind of people you ask
round for a game of cards.
They'd light up a mouse,
flick ash on the carpet and
when they left, stub it out,
lay it over their ear and look
you in the eye. And we're
all part of it – fruit and
vegetable murderers. We
even murder SALT!

An elephant and a hippopotamus discover themselves lying in adjacent cells. They spend the night discussing old days in the jungle in frantic whispers, not once mentioning their reasons for being gaolbirds.

A Young God

A myopic starling thinks I'm
a lump of fat and pecks off
my adipose till, once again, I
possess the body of a young
god. It's no worse than
acupuncture – quite pleasant
in fact. 'Thank you, birdie,' I
smile. Startled, it moves to
the edge of the balcony and
takes off, but it's 30 lbs
heavier now, so it plummets
to the grass and bursts.

Crawling worms, dying
wasps, tell me – what is the
meaning of life?
Ants, standing at the traffic
lights,
let me hear what you have
to say.
Ichneumon, leaning on the
counter at the outpatients
department of the Royal
Insect Hospital with a
blocked ovipositor, come
back in three months.

Happy Hen

The happiness of birds is
not reflected on their faces.
Strictly, birds do not have a
face – just organs around
the head. If a hen looks bad-
tempered, it is due to a
superficial disposal of its
features, and if you place
your ear by its beak, it may
well be heard humming a
contemporary dance tune in
a happy, thready fashion.

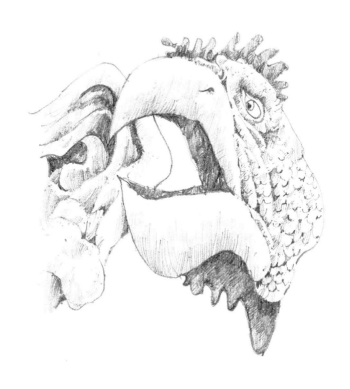

As the donkey clip-clopped through the mountains an eagle landed on his back and began eating. 'Let him,' thought the donkey, 'I have enough for two and besides my back's itchy.' The eagle, embarrassed, hopped along the spine – it had been feasting on the haunches – 'Look here,' it croaked, 'fair's fair. You have a go at me.' 'OK, birdie,' heehawed the donkey and chawed the eagle's head. The sharp beak made it taste like a thistle a bit. This symbiotic relationship continued till they reached the plain. 'See you on the way back,' croaked the big feathery scavenger.

A bison's face is its whole
head – a rueful head. It is
not grateful for having been
saved from extinction. 'You
the exterminator, and you
the preserver – man – look
much alike to me. An
uncultured mob. And you,
Mister Poet, keep your
phoney empathy. Spending
£25 on a season ticket to pop
in and feel sorry for me. Be
a pal, next time bring your
rifle. You tell all your chums
how pragmatic you are.'

Birdswing

Got a letter
from a thrush.
Come and see
me compose.
So I went.
She stuck
her beak
into the ink
and sputtered
on to the manuscript.
Then sang it.
Tra la la
tweet tweet
warble warble
ptui ptui.
When she finished
I was asked
for an opinion.
With a grave look
I opined:
Well
it's very good.
Regular thrush music
good range
plenty of variety
nice timbre.
Look Cutler
said thrush
do you think
it's worth
making a demodisc
or a tape
and
going round the agents?

I think
it's chart material.
Look thrush
I replied
it could only succeed
as a gimmick.
Yea, I suppose,
she tweeted
and flew
into a stump.

Whale Badge

A young hiker with leather
boots relieved herself in a
ditch by a remote field. It
was a disaster. She pulled
up her jeans and strode off,
singing a folksong, leaving
millions of dying organisms,
unable to cope with the
sudden change in the
composition of their
medium. It was fortunate
that she never found out,
for she cared deeply and
wore a 'Save the Whale'
badge.

Do That Again

Ever since I had wings and
landed on the table and
everybody spilled their soup
and jumped up and
shouted, I've been happy.
Do that again, said Dad. So I
did it. Then they finished
their soup and talked about
what had happened. I
landed on the ceiling and
the wall. I hovered for as
much as a minute. I even
stridulated, then hopped
across the room. It was easy
to see I had become a
favourite. Yet, when they
went to bed, I was out the
front door. And stay there,
you sneaky little thing,
called my erstwhile loving
sister. Still, there were
spiders in the corners and a
good old moth with a musty
smell.

Duck Plants

Two great ducks, around
thirty feet, sit by the moor, a
topiary achievement, one
pitched at 5°, the other 30.
The housing estate on the
Welsh border reached and
passed them. There they
are, great ducks, among
houses, choking with dust.
When I have a free day, I
cycle there and cry, a
duckling in a sports jacket.

'Brrr!' whispered the salmon as it squeezed itself out the cold tap into the sink, 'I'm frozen!' I popped it into a pot of tepid Scotch broth, head first. He polished it off. 'You haven't a drop of the hard stuff?' I poured him a generous glass of Islay malt and held his balancers as he gulped. 'Great stuff, Jimmy. Thanks a lot. Got to go. Got a date with some eggs, ye ken!' And leapt up the hot tap. I could hear him making his way through the geyser and a faint cry of 'Christ! How do I get out of here?'

I collected him later from the cistern, half-way through the ballcock valve, and ate him for tea. First time I ever got tiddly on a fish.

Daddy-Long-Legs

Nevertheless, continued the old parrot, touching my fawn raincoat with his claw, you will continue to believe me. He hopped off the sill to the ground and sidled to the dark end of the street. On an impulse, I grabbed a slice of bread and followed, hopping with a crutch. A slice of nourishing bread, I whispered and hopped back to the house. The last thing I saw was him picking daddy-long-legs from a mossy wall and holding them to the sky for a last look and to give them a bit of flavour.

A Robin and a Rhea

If all birds were disposed of
except a robin and a rhea it
would be difficult to
persuade even the gullible
that they were kin. The
robin would give you the
horse laugh. 'I'm an insect,'
he would jeer. Likewise the
rhea would find links with
the kangaroo who is not a
bird at all though seeming to
try to take off constantly.

Lunatic

Living creatures, completely
unaware of Man's immortal
soul, see him only as a
vicious destructive creature
with an infinite capacity for
making a mess, unable to
relate to the Earth and
without aesthetics. As a
dying butterfly was heard to
whisper:—

'He's a fucking lunatic!'